Let All Creation Rejoice!

Reflections on Nature

Copyright © 2023 by Rebekkah Knight

All rights reserved.
No part of this book may be reproduced or used in any manner without written permission of the copyright owner except for the use of book quotations in a book review.
For more information, address thebookclub1946@gmail.com

Scripture taken from the New King James Version®. Copyright © 1982 by Thomas Nelson. Used by permission. All rights reserved.

First paperback edition March 2023

ISBN 9798385582624

This Book is Dedicated to my Muse
Never change, my friend

Table of Contents

Part One:

Honey in My Tea	2
A Letter to My Friends	3
Fuzzy Buzzy Bee	4
The Anthem of Amaranth	4
Silly Lily	5
Flowers of the Grass	5
Viola dear	6
The Weeds Within My Garden	7
Little Ant	8
Sweet Names	9
Yellow Rose	10
Mrs. Rose	11
Sweet Peas	11
Ranunculus	12
The Lady of the Flowers	13
Polka-Dot	13
Ladybird	14
Raspberry Summer	15
End of the Day	16
Nothing Sweet as Lemonade	16

Part Two:

The Wingback Chair	18
Here at home	18
The Troublemaker	19

Homemade Cookies	20
My Evening Date	21
Sleepy Kitty	22
Trace the Pictures	23
Not One	23
In the Quiet Home	24
From Inside to Out	25

Part Three:

Peace in the Storm	28
Rainstorm on the Farm	29
Just a trace	30
Anywhere	31
The Tire Swing	32
A Rope Swing	32
Haiku in Four Seasons	33
Meadow of Dreams	33
Tulip Town	34
Alone Under Starry Skies	36
The Barn	37
Hoofbeat Tempos	38
Drafts and Ponies	38
Kwanzan in the Field	39
The Forest Meadow	40

Part Four:

The Mountain Lake	42
Lake 22	43

Painted Mountains	44
Leave No Trace	45
Row of Giants	46
Tricube of Summiting	47
Hiking Alone	47
I Never Walk with Music	48
Back in the Woods	48
Realm of Dreams	49
The Forest of Secrets	50
Mediocre Fun	51
Sunrise Over the Mountains	51
Part Five:	
Morning Wildfire	54
Little Cloud	55
Blue Skies Are No Fun	55
Commanding the Skies	56
My Favorite Sunsets	57
Ocean Sunsets	58
Part Six:	
The Wise One at the Shore	60
Great Blue Heron	62
The River	62
Salty Seas, Salty Skies	63
Gulls by the Seaside	64
Window	64
Beauty Despite Brokenness	65

Upon the Seas	66
Rocky Shores	67
George	67
Beach Remains	68
Easter at the Seaside	69
Ocean Cliffs	69
Together by the Ocean	70
Paint the World	71
Who Calmed the Seas	72
Part Seven:	
Our Shepherd is Good	74
Listen	75
In Everything, Praise	75
Unity Found	76
Haiku of Missions	76
Counting	77
A Prayer of Supplication	78
A Visual Hymn	79
Flowers at the College	81
Choose	82
Praise in Trials	82
Only	83
Praise God for Music	84
Comfort from the Stars	85
Praise God Forever!	85
Let Each One Encourage	86

Choose Joy	87
A Poem of Prayer	87
Those Who Are Blessed	88
I Know the Lord is Watching	88
Let All Things Praise the Lord	89

Part One:
In the Garden

Honey in My Tea

Honey in my Tea
Some music on my phone
Now Spring arrives, with weather warm
I rest here on my own

But I am not alone
Not really all the way
For in the sunbeams dance the bees
And here the beetles play

I read a simple book
Or sit here in sun's rays
My garden chair, like Heaven found
So now the Lord I praise

Worry can not stay
For God is present here
So even when I leave this place
I know I need not fear

So with Honey in my Tea
Some music on my phone
I worship God who molded all
This place in memory known

A Letter to My Friends

Dearest friends,

Thank you, for letting me work amongst you
Sun not yet high, blossoms gleaming with dew

As weeds are pulled and dead flowers removed
You buzz beside me and my mood is improved

Some fear your sound, or think that you will sting
But I know that thought is a silly nonsense thing

For here in the garden, we are friends, not foe
As long as I am careful, and you fly slow

So thank you, my friends, for all that you do
The world might be a duller place, were it not for you

Fuzzy Buzzy Bee

Fuzzy, buzzy, busy bee
Working hard for me
Hazy, daisy days ahead
To make the sweet honey

The Anthem of Amaranth

O flower of Amaranth now bloom in haste
Adorned triumphant in red, burgundy, gold, or green.
No flower is her equal, no spinach has her taste
She creates food and is not just a pretty thing seen

As her flower comes true, so her grain too will grow
Feed us blossom, leaf, stem, but save seed to sow

Forever we'll remember the amaranth
That grows in gardens, fields, and along the towpath

Silly Lily

Silly, frilly, chilly lily
Blooms in early spring
Hello, mellow, yellow fellow
Joyful smiles bring

Busy, squishy, wishy fishy
Named after a trout
Planted, enchanted, taken-for-granted
We love when your flowers are out

Flowers of the Grass

My lawn is made of clover, moss, and young shoots of plantain

Of tasty hairy bittercress, not much grass here remains

The dandelions with yellow hue will soon become a wish

These edible tasty little flowers will fill my salad dish

You can't deny how strange it is, that some these plants will pass

For there's a feast within my yard, the flowers of the grass

Viola dear
A reflection on flowers that keep blooming long past their season

Viola, dear
Don't you hear?
The wind that blows the trees

Viola, dear
It's drawing near
The chilly Winter breeze

Viola, dear
It's very clear
It's time to hibernate, please

The Weeds Within My Garden

There stood weeds within my garden
Who for too long had been granted pardon
So I took up their leaves
And pulled roots up with these
For against all these plants I was hardened

I ripped out the purple bugleweed
And pulled up clovers of all breed
Then I brushed off my hand
From the dirt and the sand
But neglected to watch out for seed

A week of weed-free-ness I passed then
In flower-filled, peaceful heaven
But then quite overnight
I was met with a fright
For the weeds had returned once again

So back down to garden I go now
To stop those to whom I must not bow
For the weeds will return
To my lasting concern
And to conquer them must be my vow

Little Ant

Little ant
Would you not grant
That you and I
Throw plans awry

Little beetle
Must you needle
My simple plans
Which leaf eating bans

Little ant
Upon that plant
You're quite a pest
When you digest

Little spider
You strange outsider
You're in the way
Of work and play

Little ant
Who I supplant
This is *my* yard
It's not that hard

Little wasp
Curled on the knosp
Please go away
The rest can stay

Sweet Names

"What's in a name?" the poet writes
The rose would still smell as sweet
But word's description are greatest heights
And a well-suited name a great feat

I picture rose within my mind
With soft petal and scent so kind

Sweet is a name, when called out to me
Or given in speech to another
For hearing my name just fills me with glee
When spoken by a brother

Your name is so grand when said by friend
And to heights of joy, might make me ascend

So what's in a name, you ask thus of me
I'd say the name is you
And that, my dear, if you can't see
Is something amazing and true

For you define your name as good
So love that name, I always would

Yellow Rose

Great-grandma's favorite flower was, I hear, a yellow rose
I had no chance to meet her, before her time here came to close

But every time I see them, when walking past a store
I usually stop to buy them, if only myself for

Though dahlias are my favorite to grow out in the yard
The loving of a yellow rose is one I'll always guard

Mrs. Rose

Mrs. Rose, do you suppose
Your thorns were meant for me?

Who gently pruned the suckers
That water stole from thee

Mrs. Rose, do you think those
Were meant to scratch and sting?

For such a beautiful flower
Did pack a nasty zing

Mrs. Rose, do you oppose
The clipping of your vines?

For you climbed up past rooftop
And up past your confines

Sweet Peas

Short and sweet, this poem is
Like that it is about
The trailing sweetpea on the vine
Can cheer you from a pout

The sweetpea has a lovely scent
Is cute to have around
In pinks and whites and navy blue
And others do abound

Ranunculus

There are ranunculus in my yard
I bought them quite by chance
For the tag was very marred
When I purchased the plants

They sat on discount shelf, half dead
And pity did I take
I'd no idea they'd bloom red
With centers almost fake

Some people call them buttercup
But they aren't that to me
For those I've had to clean right up
When they grow wild and free

They're "persian" buttercups I grow
Or so my big books say
But I'll just say that all I know
Is they brighten up my day

So buy the flowers at the store
That seem to be near gone
For some of them will be no bore
And may glow like the dawn

The Lady of the Flowers

She's bigger and stronger than any man around
With black lace wings and a polka-dot gown
Herself holds with grace and a regal stature
In the garden kingdom there are very few who match her

Basking in the sun when she tires of flight
Her crimson beauty is a magnificent sight
Resting on green leaf or a pale white flower
She holds us captivated by her power

Polka-Dot

Polka-dot, polka-dot
Little insect with a spot

Polka-dot, polka-dot
Love it when the weather's hot

Polka-dot, polka-dot
Tickling feet when you are caught

Polka-dot, polka-dot
Bright red elytra is what you've got

Polka-dot, polka-dot
Ladybug lot

Ladybird
A gentle request when I need my garden tools back

Mr. Ladybird
A'sitting on the hoe
Can I have a word
And ask you please to go?

Raspberry Summer

"I am the Vine," our Savior said
Words which seemed silly when I first heard them read
Of pruning and grafting I surely knew not
When I was but a tiny tot
This summer I worked with a raspberry vine
To tend and to cut and to keep as mine
It showed me the lesson of cutting out rot
To prepare the vine for the fruit it brought
Apart from the vine, the branches soon died
And couldn't bear fruit even if they tried
So praise God for the teaching of the raspberry summer
And for vine metaphors in which understanding can occur

End of the Day

The day has finally come to close
And twilight's last breath strokes the rose
Tomorrow we'll begin once more
To pull the weeds that we abhor

But for tonight, our rest is won
The flowers planting all is done
Nighttime beauty is our prize
As in shadows, garden lies

Nothing Sweet as Lemonade

There's nothing sweet as lemonade, once the work is done
Nothing like a home made snack, after race is won

When all is finished, all is said, we'll rest inside our home
The war of beauty ever runs, in dirt and sand and loam

But we must all take time to rest, when the day is through
For work will always come on back, when tomorrow's new

Part Two:
Around the House

The Wingback Chair

Work is long and sometimes sad, but when home I've returned
I'm greeted by the wingback chair, and quiet that's been earned

It's here in books that I get lost, with tea to sip as well
Beside me on the end table, a candle with sweet smell

Though this is not my dream house, and life is far from grand
I rejoice in the simple things, and all that God has planned

For sitting in my wingback chair, away from all the noise
My mind can be at rest as I reflect on little joys

Here at home

Here at home, my mind at ease
Here my tired brain appease

Rest within a Bible verse
Let your worries then disperse

Here at home, a peace of mind
Seek the Lord and you shall find

The Troublemaker

I know a little troublemaker
Innocent though he seems
You can see it in his eyes
The ideas that he schemes

He fools you with cuteness
His sweet little gaze
But if given a chance
The house he will raze

When he's in all his bedding
All burrowed inside
Something suspicious
What he tries to hide

Red-handed not caught yet
I've not had the luck
I know a little troublemaker
His name is Chuck

Homemade Cookies

Homemade cookies and homemade bread
Cooked up from the recipes I read

My skills might not be perfect, the shortbread may fall flat
And sometimes what I've baked is not too pretty to look at

Homemade cookies and homemade pies
Leaving dough in a bowl to rise

Though my baked treats are simple, and often not fancy
They're plenty good enough to be gobbled by family

Homemade cookies and homemade tarts
Molasses cookies and candy hearts

The frosting uneven, the pattern slightly off
But when it comes to eating them, my family doesn't scoff

Homemade cookies and homemade bread
Cooked up from the recipes I read

My Evening Date

My man dresses in a fine tuxedo
Around his neck a bow
He looks so smart most every night
When off to dinner we go

His bright green eyes are filled with light
He's a handsome sight
He greets me at the door at home
My man is my handsome knight

He likes with me to read a tome
He will never roam
I know his love is not remote
Nor quickly lost like the seafoam

I think it could be worth a note
About what I have wrote
My "man" is really just a cat
Upon whom I like to dote

Sleepy Kitty

Curled up in my blankets when I tried to leave for work
Morning came a while ago, yet still in sleep you lurk

Sleepy kitty watch the time, I really need to leave
And leave you in the room cannot, or dead plants I'll receive

You're so at peace upon the bed, I hate to kick you out
But if I leave you here all day, there cannot be a doubt

That trouble will be caused by you, when finally are awake
So sleepy little kitty, from the bed I take

Trace the Pictures

Trace the pictures you can't paint
And the mistakes please don't hate

Everybody has their skill
Some hands shake with other's still

Beauty comes in many sizes
And from each talent arises

But if drawing's not your skill
Yet the pictures bring you thrill

Trace the pictures you can't paint
Don't let challenge be restraint

Not One

A reminder that you are loved and you do great things, even if you aren't the world's best at that thing

Not one is perfect but God, my dear
Don't kill yourself trying to be
One who never a mistake does make
Darling, you're worrying me

Not one is perfect but God, my dear
That doesn't mean I won't love
Things you enjoy even if you're not "great"
It's no matter the quality they're of

In the Quiet Home

Raindrops on my window
A kitty is on my lap
The curtains have been pulled aside
But I'm ready for a nap

Sitting in my rocker
Curled up with my fav'rite book
The sounds of purring fills my ears
As I'm settled in this nook

The reading wakes me up
As grand journies I do trace
My English tea is piping hot
So anything I can face

Here with raindrops on my window
And a kitty still on my lap
I've here and now excitement reached
There's no further risk of nap

From Inside to Out

When house has been cleaned up
Both inside and out
My heart is so glad that I'm sure I could shout

When chores are all finished
And it's time to rest
I take pleasure in knowing that I did my best

Tomorrow's the weekend
So when early I'll rise
To see the bright colors a'crossing the skies

And I head out hiking
With family or friends
For that is the way I like spending weekends

Monday we'll restart
With chores all about
And fix up our home again, from inside to out

Part Three:
Farm and Field

Peace in the Storm

Meadow of gold under a dark blue sky
Soon the thunder will supply

A rolling wave of rumblings
To silence all my grumblings

Out here you can feel the power
Of One who made Earth, sea, and flower

And all my fears He does supplant
Eternal calm and peace does grant

But when strongest lightning charge
Cross the sky appears in large
Now is time to go inside
From the lightning we must hide

For the beauty of the storm
From a place of danger formed

Watching through the window panes
Rain that sweeps across the plains

With a smile on my face
Though my heart begins to race

Excitement mounts with thunder's crash
Following the lightning flash

So I make a cup of tea
And with sense of jubilee

From my chair aside the fire
Watch the storm until I tire

Sleeping then within my chair
Curled up as the cat does snare

Place within my lap to stay
Til the storm does blow away

There is peace within the storm
If new perspective you do form

Rainstorm on the Farm

Drip drop, drop drip
Rain outside the door
Tick tock, tock tick
Clock is chiming four

Clip clop, clop clip
Horses in the barn
Drip drop, drop drip
Rainstorm on the farm

Just a trace

It snowed the other day my dear, a few inches on the grass
But not enough to block the streets or close Snoqualmie pass

Down here in the lowlands, it was a lovely sight
Looking at the blanket of crisp and pure bright white

There upon the surface of a canvas almost untouched
I saw a trace of prints there, where robin's feet had brushed

Anywhere

If I could take you anywhere, I'd find a field of flowers
For there you might find calm and rest that are beyond my powers

The sweetest scent of lavender or roses on the breeze
And if I could, I'd wish away your pollen allergies

You're stuck inside, and that's no good. Please just come outside
The world will keep on going, even if you hide

If I could take you anywhere, I'd take you to the valley
Come on, right now, I'll drag you there, if smidge of strength you rally

My friend, you've stayed at home too long, that can't be good for you
I know you like it here indoors, but outside is good too

If I could take you anywhere, we'd go down to the river
Just put some faith in God above, from fear He will deliver

The Tire Swing

I see it in my mind when thinking of my friends
As though the memory's captured and it never ends

I wasn't even present, when that picture was caught
And that's how I prefer it, almost as if forgot

They stand around a tire swing, posing for the pic
Some of them are grinning, as if up to some trick

The summer sky is cloudy, though the day was hot
Only two are missing, of the friends I've got

Though not at all nearby, in some city unknown
The tire swing reminds me that I am not alone

A Rope Swing

My friend's house was built by a hill
A long and sloping thing
Great maples stood against the rise
And one branch held rope swing

If you did grab from summit there
The robe within your grasp
You'd just then swing but don't let go
For to ground would be 12 feet past

Haiku in Four Seasons

At last, Spring arrives
Showcasing flowers of grass
Wet dew and young life

Heat draws close, sun burns
Beach days, ice water, milk shakes
Summer comes then ends

Rain and leaves, Autumn
Bright colors float on the wind
Frosty mornings here

Winter blows around
Red cheeks and sparkling laughs
Lights adorn the house

Meadow of Dreams

Dark clouds fill sky above
Golden wheat dance, anticipation
Rush of wind and rain

Tulip Town

There within the meadow, nestled in the hills
Sits a tulip farm, without too many frills

Just row and row of flowers, with gravel at their feet
And in this little tulip town, tulips you will meet

There are a couple daffodils, but they are not the star
It's because of tulips the tourists come from far

The flowers sit in long bright rows, all arranged by color
Like little tulip families, with mom and sis and brother

I saw a tulip while there, and he did catch my eye
For he was a bit taller in reaching for the sky

Amongst the ivory tulips, yet he was clothed in pink
Of growing far away from friends, he didn't seem to think

I love my little tulip friend, so different as he were
For even though not quite alike, it didn't cause a stir

Alone Under Starry Skies

I walk alone under starry skies
The wind is cold and the field is wide
Yet I do not think yet to go inside
As I watch stars shift before my eyes

The grasses crunch with the icy frost
I slowly drift as I look above
And with the sky seem to be in love
But tear gaze away lest I soon be lost

I trudge cross the meadow, though I pause to look
At the starry skies in their cloudless night
The moon so wane as to not cast light
And for brief moments it's like I'm in a book

But back to Earth I must turn my thought
To the walk ahead through silent wood
Yet to watch forever, I know I could
Now to get back home I surely ought

The field is dim and thick grasses wave
Even frogs and crickets now do hide
And now I think I'll go inside
For way out here I'm not always brave

The Barn

I have a barn that's in my head
A wondrous place of dreams
For though a horse I can't afford
In memory my mount gleams

Can something like this memory be called
For there I've never been
But hope one day to find self there
Though I have no thought when

The barn is lined with eight wide stalls
I've just finished my chores
I've mucked the place and waters filled
And swept the tack room floors

There's hard work in this memory place
Yet I still call it rest
For in the barn amongst the steeds
Is what I like the best

Six stalls are filled with my horses
And two are there for guests
The birds in rafters sing and fly
And barn cats fight off pests

Hoofbeat Tempos

The horse trotting down the lane is
Up down bouncing tempo is his

My horses that canter about in their pen
Move around as graceful as does fly the wren

Then we gallop, flying so fast
Wind in our hair, worries now past

Finally we walk back to the barn
Nestled beside the woods and the tarn

Drafts and Ponies

Gentle giant in the field
Misunderstood is he
Though he stands at 18 hands
He's always kind to me

The ponies are the ones to watch
Those devilish little things
Don't ever on them turn your back
For all of them, trouble brings

Kwanzan in the Field

Waiting for my family, I wandered through the park
The contrast of pink flowers against the greyish bark

The flowers were quite frilly, like fancy petticoats
And colors were so pretty, I wrote it in my notes

With photo of the blossoms, and a notebook with their traits
I opened up my garden books, which therein recreates

So many different flowers, but I soon found thereupon
The flowers growing in the park are cherries called Kwanzan

The Forest Meadow

There's a spot in the forest, a meadow within
Where something just like an adventure begins

If picnic you're having, or just out there to read
Stay quiet and to your surroundings heed

For out of the woods, the deer will come
One can not say quite where from

And if gentle and quiet you still remain
From quick movements do refrain

They will let you follow, if careful you are
To lost forest meadows that thickets do bar

I cannot follow deer that far, though I wish I might
For my cat is missing me, and it is almost night

Part Four:
Mountains and Forests

The Mountain Lake

Mountain lake, mountain lake
Why are you here?
Mountain lake, mountain lake
Water so clear

Mountain lake, mountain lake
Summer has come
Mountain lake, mountain lake
Here we'll have fun!

Lake 22

The lake seems fake in photos
So gently picturesque
But I've been there in person
It helps me see I'm blessed

For even when I can't afford
A house or fancy clothes
I need only to hike up there
To see how goodness flows

In seeing such a pretty place
I can't imagine why
There's people on this precious world
Who don't trust God on High

It is beside the lake
Or in forests or the park
I see His hand created all
That fact to me is stark

So when I'm feeling doubtful
Or like nobody cares
I'll head back to the lake
And breath the mountain airs

Painted Mountains

I put my brush upon the page
And with broad strokes I made
A sky with bluish painted hues
And sunset pinks displayed

Then mountains against the twilight
Grew before my eyes
So naturally were they then formed
That I was most surprised

In pinks and blacks and blues I saw
The snowy faces form
Though hardly made realistically
Emotion seemed to swarm

I felt as though I really there
Could feel the rocky space
And though if canvas I did touch
I'd travel to that place

I'm no good painter, that I know
For words are more my craft
But in that little piece of art
I feel the summit's draft

Leave No Trace

Enter the forest wisely, love
Go out with what you came
Protect dear nature's beauty
Or she'll never be the same

The trees are sturdy, mostly
But they can damage too
The only thing they ask for
Respectfulness from you

This is the home of plants, yes
And birds and beasts and fish
To treat their dwelling kindly
Is all that they would wish

If trash you find along the path
Or clutter in the park
Compassion have, and pick it up
For the forest feels the mark

To keep this place protected, love
It is our holy call
We must take care of the forest
Or into ruin it will fall

So when you seek to wander
To find solace in this place
Please don't disturb the flowers
We ask you, leave no trace

Row of Giants

Row of giants, standing tall
Three of them are shown in all

Lord, we pray they never fall
Row of giants, standing tall

Path of mountains in a row
In the sunlight, how you glow

Glisten white with ice and snow
Path of mountains in a row

Dotted summits in a path
May we never face your wrath

Cascade range with such peaks hath
Dotted summits in a path

Tricube of Summiting

Standing proud
Summit peak
Trees below

Strange feeling
Victory
Reached top

Down from here
We must go
Tired walk

Hiking Alone

Hiking alone
My favorite way
That I could think
To spend a day

Hiking alone
In peace and still
A quiet time
In this I thrill

Hiking alone
Will always be
The way that I
Will feel I'm free

I Never Walk with Music

I never walk with music on when I am in the wood
Instead I drink in all the sounds around me that I could

The birds that sing amongst the trees, gravel on the ground
The world is filled with quiet noise, and I embrace the sound

I never hike with music on, when forest I explore
For I would never want to miss the adventure that's in store

Back in the Woods

Back in the woods, among the trees
Where gravel turns to dirt
The path is quite less trodden here
At least, that's what I've learnt

This is where I love to sit
Beside a trickling creek
I go to the forest to find my peace
When I am feeling bleak

Here in the forest, all is calm
And here I feel close to God
So hiking is a rest for me
Is that so very odd?

Realm of Dreams

Deep in fog the forest lay
Not all is what it seems
For here the clouds by tree trunks play
We're in the realm of dreams

Whispery tendrils swirl around
Silhouetted are the trees
In shadowed quiet on the ground
The forest sits at ease

Though it's still and quiet here
And things might seem quite tense
I know that I need not fear
For the forest's my defense

The Forest of Secrets

The forest of secrets was where we would go
To play around in days of old
What was the secret? We didn't know
But call it secret, we uphold

The place was always lit so bright
The memory of it is even light

The forest of secrets was where we would play
With birds in the trees and leaves of gold
And loneliness was kept at bay
Our fears together were consoled

Gone forever the secret now
Perhaps because we forgot how

The forest of secrets was only for kids
Who fearless wandered in the trees
I guess that's why it now us bids
To leave the past behind us please

The forest of secrets is secret still
And ne'er again will we there find thrill

Mediocre Fun

When I say I like to hike
There are many who do say
That they could never be good enough
To go and hike all day

When I say I love great ships
Or kayaking to go
There are many who will say
That they simply do not know

But I don't hike because I'm good
At kayaking not number one
I do these things because of love
This "mediocre" fun

Sunrise Over the Mountains

Sunrise over the mountains
Must be a thrilling thing
It's as if you are watching
A holy choir sing

Sunrise over the mountains
When out amongst the wild
Is something that I haven't seen
Since I was but a child

Part Five:
The Skies Above

Morning Wildfire

Darkness
Silence but for the wind
Early
The morning not yet come

Dawn
The shadows thinned
Bright
The starlight must succumb

Pink
Background for the trees
Orange
A base of light is formed

Fire
Break through silhouetted leaves
Color
Witness sunrise's reward

Little Cloud

Little cloud, you're rather loud
For one who makes no sound

But in deep blue, and blackish hue
And slightly silver crowned

Little cloud, you're rather mad
For one who has no face

Your color makes you seem upset
As others join the space

Little cloud, you are quite grim
For such a little thing

But when with friends are gathering
Then thunderstorm you bring

Blue Skies Are No Fun

Blue skies are no fun
If you were asking me
All you get to see is sun
And I just feel grumpy

Cloudy days are best
If color you prefer
Blueish grey the skies impress
Wouldn't you concur?

Commanding the Skies

If the skies I could command, and always have my way
I'd give us often starry nights, with ever cloudy days

So we could watch the ISS or comets going past
And gaze into the starlight sky that is so very vast

Rain would fall most every day, watering the plants
But for growth it'd still be bright, that at much I'll grant

Temps would never be too hot, not over seventy
Then again, I soon would make, more than one enemy

I guess there is a reason why God controls the sky
For there would not be balance, if changed it all did I

My Favorite Sunsets

The stormy weather sunset
Is my favorite thing
A special kind of sunset
That has a quite nice ring

I made the name up one day
When driving home from work
And I guess one could say
A storm had come to lurk

The skies were dark almost across
Except for in the West
So everything glowed golden
And I'm sure you guess the rest

The yellowed trees with backdrop blue
Just seem to somehow shine
Though most like pink or orangey hue
The stormy kind is mine

So next time dark clouds start to brew
But clear skies grace the West
Dwell longer on the sky's view
And see what I like best

Ocean Sunsets

Living on the East coast
You never get to see
A proper type of sunset
Where it sets across the sea

The sunrise is fantastic
Especially with the sound
Of all the waking birds
Singing all around

But in an ocean sunset
A peaceful lack of strife
As into night time we descend
And stars all come to life

Praise God for ocean sunsets
Though there are far away
The beauty of creation
In sunsets is displayed

Part Six:
The Waters Below

The Wise One at the Shore

Amongst the rocks, along the shore
There sits the one who knows much more
Than any else who you might ask
But first you must get past his mask

He has much knowledge, from 'round the globe
And huddled in his thick grey robe
He'll mentor you, if worthy are
And teach you things from near and far

His manner stiff, his voice is gruff
One might say he is quite rough
For years of living by the sea
Have hardened heart towards you and me

But speaking of his only love
The ocean's fish or crabs thereof
A salty voice will tell you then
His self be brought alive again

So if knowledge of the ocean is what you seek
Head down to the beach, but don't be too meek
Ask for the Heron who sits on the rock
And the sailors will tell you which way to walk

Great Blue Heron

Great Blue Heron, lord of the Sound
Resting in a marsh
Great Blue Heron, king of around
Even when weather harsh

I looked out on an icy land
What did I see
Great Blue Heron, in the snow
Sleeping happily

The River

The river that flows through the wandering wood
Always never follows the path that it should

For it twists off to one side, then turns back around
And weaves aimless through trees, with babbling sound

Sit by the lost river is all that I ask
And through filtered sunlight, here we can bask

Salty Seas, Salty Skies

Salty seas with salty skies
Cold wind blowing in my eyes

Waves that splash while lions bark
Tides that wash away your mark

Sea shells, beach glass, kelp around
Tiny treasures that I've found

Salty seas with salty skies
Currents rush in calm that lies

Water breaks against the rocks
Fisherman cast from off the docks

Off the coast, the great ships sit
Overhead the seagulls flit

Salty seas with salty skies
Swells begin to grow and rise

In the rock's pools, creatures hide
Waiting for the coming tide

Clouds begin to rumble in
Now is not the time to swim

Salty seas with salty skies
Just the place for last goodbyes

Gulls by the Seaside

Clashing waves, within the caves
That echo through the skies
Rushing in, then pouring out
While overhead, seagulls fly

Knowing not a reason yet
They try to race the sea
But always fail, though try again
A strange mystery to me

They dive towards the water's edge
And plunge beneath the wave
To find a dinner meant to eat
Then fly beyond the cave

Window

My window to the ocean
My place beside the sea
Is like a balm or lotion
When life's too hard for me

I pull my rocking chair there
When too cold to go outside
And dream of summer days where
I'll go and kayak ride

Beauty Despite Brokenness

Cracked and broken though she lay
Upon the sandy beach
I took no notice of the lack
When she was in my reach

Upon tan sand, a striking brown
With speckled pink and white
This little, broken half of shell
Was precious in my sight

Forbidden was from beach to take
So left it all alone
But captured beauty I did keep
In picture on my phone

Upon the Seas

I could live upon a boat and sail upon the sea
And wouldn't ever feel alone, even if 'twere only me

And under darkest midnight skies, with water black below
I'd look upon the heavens bright, and watch the universe glow

If I could live upon a boat, and sail upon the sea
My fears would be a different kind, of that I can foresee

For out upon the oceans, love, dangers are around
And hardly can you just believe that you are safe and sound

The work is hard, I'll grant you that, and bitter is the cold
But I will sail upon the seas, when I am grey and old

Rocky Shores

Cloudy skies and rocky shores
Those are the beaches I look for
While sand is soft and seems unique
Rocky tidepools are what I see

The beaches that I sometimes roam
To me are like my second home
Though I cannot see them much
They're the places I long to touch

George

There was a crab upon the beach
When last I chanced to go
As small as my thumbnail was this new friend
But he certainly wasn't slow

He made his way across the rocks
Into tiny salty pools
And moved in water as quick as above
For him there were no rules

I named him George, because why not
My tiny little friend
And see him again, I doubt I will
But my delight in him will not end

Beach Remains

The crab claw
At the beach
Left behind

Beautiful
Even loss
In this place

Against rock
There it sits
Forgotten

Easter at the Seaside

I'd love to spend Easter along the beach
For height of joy my heart does reach
And the mirth of the day my soul does preach
I'd love to spend Easter along the beach

I'd love to spend Easter upon the sand
For there I might understand the land
Where King washed disciples' feet with His own hand
I'd love to spend Easter upon the sand

I'd love to spend Easter on boat, aboard
That to me would be a reward
To understand storms that were calmed by my Lord
I'd love to spend Easter on boat, aboard

I'd love to spend Easter beside the sea
And recall the Savior who died for me
To praise Him and give Him all jubilee
I'd love to spend Easter beside the sea

Ocean Cliffs

I love the smell of salty breeze
As ocean winds blow through the trees
Rocky beaches call to me
As ocean cliffs stand wild and free

Together by the Ocean

Take me to the ocean, let's gaze upon the sea
We'll watch the rosy sunset 'til the last light seems to flee

I'll close my eyes to listen to the lapping of the waves
For even just the sound a mental picture it paves

Let's dance beside the ocean, twirling in sweet harmony
Forever let us praise the Lord, that you are here with me

Paint the World

If I could paint the world for you
A million places I would do
The highest hills, the deepest valleys
The brightest clouds and the darkest trees

And then my darling, you might see
Just how much you mean to me

If I could paint the world for you
The skies would always be so blue
The forests and the lakes are calling
And motionless the leaves are falling

So my dearest, don't you see
Just how much you mean to me

If I could paint the world for you
The places with the best of view
The greatest mounts, the meekest hollows
The calm and then the storm that follows

Now beloved, you must see
Just how much you mean to me

Who Calmed the Seas

There is only One above
With power to stop a storm
He commanded it to stop
And it did conform

Out upon the ocean waves
Who can calm the seas
For though many, ocean braves
Storm they could not freeze

Growing waves like skyscrapers
Ships do crest the swell
Prideful boast, the gale tapers
Squall could be death knell

Rejoice, oh Earth, for God on High
He who calmed the seas
Paid for sins when came to die
For the least of these

Storms are powerful in grade
But He is Lord of all
For through Him the world was made
What challenge is a squall?

Part Seven:
Psalms, Hymns, and Spiritual Songs

Our Shepherd is Good
A reflection and response to Psalm 23

The Lord is always my Good Shepherd
I know I shall not be in want
This comfort given from His true Word
Helps me dwell on Him at the front

He makes me lie down in green pastures
Beside the still waters He leads
These words spoken still by our pastors
In good times and harsh ones, it feeds

My soul is restored by Him only
He in paths of righteousness will guide
And if ever I feel I am lonely
I'll remember He is by my side

Though I walk through a valley of evil
A place of the shadow of death
Though things seem to be in upheaval
I know I'm sustained by His breath

Surely goodness and mercy will follow
For all of the days of my life
His promises never are hollow
In His house there will never be strife

Listen

Listen
From us, a demand, an order
A command, a cry to another

Listen
Spoken out when we refuse to hear
To no avail we try making "truth"

Listen
A soft request, a whispered voice
Beckoning for us to lay down steel tongue

Listen
A choice remains for you to make
Follow the Truth or make your own way

In Everything, Praise

Praise God in sunshine, praise Him in rain
Praise Him when blessings do not seem plain

Praise God in hardship, praise Him in good
Praise Him when others don't think that you should

Praise God in Summer, Spring, Winter, and Fall
Praise when you can't think of praises at all

Unity Found

Unity is found in the gospel
The faith in Christ our Lord
Without Him things always unravel
And dissension becomes our reward

When we lose sight of Who has saved us
If we let law and symbol be first
Then we aren't living by His instruction
And our church or groups will disperse

We need to hang on to His promise
For God is the One who supplies
Keeping daily in mind all His teachings
Then His wisdom will be no surprise

Haiku of Missions

> Lord, we lift our song
> Equip and send on Your mission
> Let us shine as lights

Counting

Count
Your blessings
As they come
Don't forget them soon

For every good gift
Comes from above
And freely
Strewn

Patience
My friend
You will see
He's all you need

The Word He sent
To give life
And plant
Seeds

A Prayer of Supplication
Inspired by the psalms of David

Lord, give me faith to stand for You
In trials I cannot last without Your hand
Though I falter You are always true
Your grace and mercy fill tumultuous land

Through good times and bad I have anxieties
Teach me, Lord, to lean on Your support
For difficulties have their many varieties
And my own strength will always fall short

You, our God, are the only holy One
We tried to rule our fates, but never could
Over sin and death, it's You who won
And by Your Son, we can again be good

Thank You, Lord, for all that You have made
Help us to remember it's Your story
It was You by whom sin's price was paid
Let all my actions be to Your glory

So lead my life according to Your plan
Trials of the world please help me fight
You who existed before time began
You who are our perfect guiding light

Amen

A Visual Hymn

Crystal clear waters touch sandy white beach
The oceans I've seen only in my dreams
A tropical refuge where troubles can't reach
Within memory this lovely place seems

Though go there I have not, nor in future near
I picture it clearly, as if I had been
This place in my thoughts I will always hold dear
And pretend I can go there when troubles begin

The Lord of Creation, the Master of seas
Can gentle peace bring like the island of vision
He speaks just a word and anxiety flees
What I only imagine, He created with precision

Praise Him Who created the greatest and least
For His holy name we create pale shadow of glory
By the Lord's righteousness, we are increased
As we work and we live to follow His story

So I count it all joy to become more like Him
And imagine my peaceful ocean as a visual hymn

Flowers at the College

The flowers at the college
Are beauty near the war
Though this a place of knowledge
Their wisdom's very poor

So many lost here wander
With spiritual neglect
They've turned from God the Father
Their own fates to direct

They worship knowledge freely
Instead of Him who gives
And have turned so completely
Disbelieve the King who lives

All the beauty growing here
Covers how they aren't free
For deep down they live in fear
Of a loss they cannot see

Why can't we just acknowledge
The pretty things are a ruse
The flowers at the college
Might as well just be refuse

Choose

Do you trust in God or are the enemy of God?
Choose

Are you a peacemaker or are you "always" right?
Choose

Do you recognize that all us are flawed
And by perfect Lord we should all be awed?

Do you oft forgive or take path of spite?
Choose

Praise in Trials
A praise to God for being good in the hard times

Lord, we praise you for these trials!
For in these things we will grow
Though at this time, it may seem to discourage
The plans for what is best you always know

You shape us like a potter at a clay wheel
And each of us are crafted and unique
We couldn't ask for a more loving Father
And equally You help the strong and weak

Only

Only
One way to the Father
On that day considered it no bother

Only
No other way might be found
Nothing could separate once we were brought round

Only
Love shown in its greatest
Life everlasting came through the plainest

Only
You, Lord our God, have saved us
Yearning we come to You who makes us righteous

Only
Jesus, the Way, the Truth, the Life

Praise God for Music

Praise God for music
For rhythm and flow
Whether acoustic
With lyrics or no

Praise God for harmony
Both dissonant and pure
For those singing heartily
Or those small but clear

Praise God for sonnets
For rhyme and for verse
For in and upon it
A song does transverse

Rejoice in the music
For all that it is
Praise God for the music
The glory is His

Comfort from the Stars

Who could ever claim that the stars were accident
Some might think it true, but my knowledge is intransigent

For looking up into the sky, in all its starlit glory
It's evident they were all placed by He who writes this story

Patterns endlessly intricate, with nebulae and stars
Planets dancing round their suns, like Goldilocks or Mars

These could never come about by accident or luck
Each was placed with purpose, by God they there were stuck

So if you're ever doubtful of how much you might mean
Take comfort from the stars, and in Him who made them seen

Praise God Forever!

Praise God forever! He is our Lord
Thank Him that death will not be our reward
Praise God forever! The King of all Kings
Praise God for His Son, salvation brings!

Let Each One Encourage

Let each one encourage the other
As children of God we are brother and sister
Share the love of Christ with another

All of our sins He did cover
Over death He was the victor
Let each one encourage the other

Teach yourselves to love your brother
Even when disagreements are bitter
 Share the love of Christ with another

The light of God let no one smother
Before speaking be the listener
Let each one encourage the other

Sometimes in patience we should suffer
Then won't fall to the Resister
Share the love of Christ with another

Practice grace and you'll discover
From the body we'll not splinter
Let each one encourage the other
Share the love of Christ with another

Choose Joy

Choose Joy
James reminds us of this fact

Choose Joy
No easy task is this call

Choose Joy
Joy will not always just come

Choose Joy
You must make the decision

Choose Joy
Choose Life
Choose Jesus

A Poem of Prayer

Lord we praise You for Your grace
From us please don't hide Your face

We ask for mercy in our faults
For protection from evil's assaults

We confess to You that we have sinned
And that our love has often thinned

Let Your Kingdom come at last
Lord, please always hold us fast

Those Who Are Blessed

Blessed are the tired, the sick, the poor
Blessed are the ones who look forward to more
This Earth will pass and He will create new
Blessed is the One who will reign after and before

Blessed are the missionaries, pastors, and teachers
Blessed are the faithful, God honoring preachers
Our God is great, His promises true
Blessed is the everlasting Redeemer

I Know the Lord is Watching

From greatest mount to deepest sea
I know the Lord is watching me

He will not lead where He can't sustain
And in His peace we shall remain

From mournful place to jubilee
I know the Lord is watching me

Let all sing praise, be filled with joy
Let all us work, as in His employ

In hardest times, may I still see
And know the Lord is watching me

Let All Things Praise the Lord
Psalm 150

Praise the Lord!
Praise God in His sanctuary;
Praise Him in His mighty firmament!

Praise Him for His mighty acts;
Praise Him according to His excellent greatness!

Praise Him with the sound of the trumpet;
Praise Him with the lute and harp!

Praise Him with the timbrel and dance;
Praise Him with stringed instruments and flutes!

Praise Him with loud cymbals;
Praise Him with clashing cymbals!

Let everything that has breath praise the Lord.
Praise the Lord!

Made in the USA
Monee, IL
20 March 2023